SEEDS OF LOVE

Being the

GLASTONBURY SERIES OF SHORT PRAYERS

by

GILBERT SHAW

Edited and Revised

in 1978 by

SISTER EDNA MONICA SLG

SLG PRESS
Convent of the Incarnation
Fairacres   Oxford
OX4 1TB

© THE SISTERS OF THE LOVE OF GOD 1978

ISBN 0 7283 0070 2
ISSN 0307-1405

*The photograph used for the cover was among a series taken by
the author, Father Gilbert Shaw*

You sow a word
  which will lie hidden . . .

At the right moment
  the word will germinate . . .
and become the full expression
  of the seed you gave,
    O divine Sower.

> George Appleton, *The Word is the Seed*

My Lord, my God, my Life, my All,
You are both the Sower
  and the Seed sown in our hearts.

> Gilbert Shaw, 'The Increase of Prayer'

PREFACE

The Glastonbury Series of Short Prayers, arranged by Gilbert Shaw and published by Faith Press, have long been out of print. They were originally compiled in answer to requests from theological colleges and retreat houses, and they were dedicated to Glastonbury which, as probably one of the oldest sites of Christian devotion in this island, had a very special appeal for Father Gilbert Shaw.

Preparation for republication began simply with the idea of transposing them into the 'you' form of address to God. However, as they were prayed over, some of the original phrases were expanded and some of Father Gilbert's very concentrated imagery and metaphor 'unpacked'. Also, in general, changing to the more direct 'you' form seemed to invite a more direct use of Scripture in some places where there was previously only an allusion to it. Father Gilbert never intended that one should adhere slavishly to his words when using them for prayer so that the degree of freedom which has been exercised in this revision is being faithful to his purpose in first writing these prayers. It is also hoped that this revision will make these prayers more readily useful to Christians whose whole liturgical language has undergone a radical alteration since the time when they were first written.

In his later years Father Gilbert took exception to the term 'mental prayer' if it was understood in too narrow a way, with a too cerebral connotation. He always emphasised, however, the need for prayer to be 'ordered' and warned against drifting into a state of reverie and absence of mind which is totally different from the absorbed attention of the 'prayer of quiet'.

But having realised that prayer is not just to be a 'mental' activity but is to engage our whole being, body, soul and spirit, we need to approach it with humility recognising that, if words are our normal vehicle of expression, they will probably have some part to play in our prayer. Pre-eminently we are given the words of the Scriptures and Liturgy to form the basis of our prayer but Father Gilbert compiled these prayers for those who do not find it easy to formulate their own affirmations directly from the Scriptures for use in affective prayer. He intended that each should use them in his or her own way, with a great freedom, so that the words could become their own.

When we come to our prayer we can begin by recalling our relationship with the Persons of the Trinity and we may read quite a long section of the prayers slowly and quietly, giving them our full attention. Gradually, as our minds are able to drop what has previously engaged their attention, and as we become still and attentive to God, we may find ourselves using just one phrase or one word to affirm our relationship and to recall our attention to him, gently, if it begins to wander. The words may even drop away completely, but they will have served their purpose in first holding our attention and directing our wills so that we may come to rest in a loving longing for and dependence upon God.

EDNA MONICA SLG
Fairacres 1978

ACKNOWLEDGEMENT

The Word is the Seed, by Bishop George Appleton, was published by SPCK in 1976 and the quotation from it used on the page following the title is taken, by kind permission, from p.35

THE INCREASE OF PRAYER

CHRIST TEACHES US in the Gospel that we should 'keep on praying and never lose heart', and he also gives us the firm promise that, 'everyone who asks receives, he who seeks finds, and to him who knocks, the door will be opened.' (Luke 18:1 and 11:10.)

Our experience, however, is that not only do we lose heart and fail to persevere, but at times we seem not even to know how to begin to pray. This is where a wider appreciation of the place of vocal prayer can be a very great help for, as Saint Teresa taught, simple vocal prayer made with full attention can bring us to union with God; but it is important that we 'think what we are asking and recognise that God is with us'. (*The Way of Perfection*, XXIX:6.)

Prayer is first of all a response to the love of God and we need to respond with all our capacities: with the reverence of our bodies, the perceptions and thoughts of our minds, the movement of our emotions and the setting and direction of our wills. We live in time and space and therefore we move in an ordered way from one thing to another. We recognise form and think in symbols and, moreover, we can use words intelligibly to communicate with one another. This same ordered process and use of words and symbols has a rightful place in our prayer and communication with God.

We have to seek, and to seek implies an element of knowledge of what is to be sought. We need to discover the meaning of what has been revealed to our minds—that God is—and that our fragmentary moment of time is before God. Prayer is a rational process and not an aimless emotional craving. It is grounded in faith, and faith is an activity of the intelligence which perceives that which is and will be, though as yet not fully understood or rationally discernible.

We seek in order to find; we have to make real what our mind has perceived. We have to realise ourselves in relationship with God as his creatures, totally dependent on him. With the knowledge that 'God made us for himself' comes our penitence, for we see where we have failed to depend on him. As we grow in dependence we find God renews our courage so that we can persevere thankfully on the way, in hope.

To begin with we have to make prayer with our mind and our will. We must provide a stimulus to move our will, otherwise we shall not be praying. Our business is to bring our minds back to God so that, working with the Holy Spirit, in the simplicity of true children of God, we can say, 'Abba, Father'. In this way our prayer, which is a response to the Love that first loved us, will find its accomplishment in the full relationship of the flow and reflow of love. Prayer will become for us our very life, for ultimately the purpose of our life is not only to make prayer but to become prayer.

SEEK

GOD, unchangeable, without beginning or end,
    you are all-sufficient, utterly perfect and infinite.
Eternal and Uncreated, you have created all that is.
My God, I love you, I adore and worship you,
    I am your creature, the work of your hands,
        hear your creature cry, Lord have mercy.

GOD, Everlasting and Almighty, you are present everywhere,
    all things speak of you and yet they cannot contain you.
You are the source of all that is good,
    and in you all good is found,
        what then can I desire in comparison with you?
God, you are all my desire. I have said,
    'You are my God, my goods are nothing to you',
    for you are my only good,
        hear your creature cry, Lord have mercy.

GOD, you are the Lord of all things, Sustainer of the universe.
    In your hands, O Lord, lie all things,
        and there is none that can resist your will.
For you, O God, have made everything,
    heaven and earth and all that is in them;
you are the Lord of Creation,
        hear your creature cry, Lord have mercy.

GOD, my heart is restless until it rests wholly in you.
    Increase my faith that I may seek and find.
You are indeed a hidden God,
    yet you reveal yourself in all your creatures.
    You choose to be hidden within my heart,
        the very Temple where you dwell,
    revealing yourself in the depth and height of my life.
O Lord, forgive my blindness, my preoccupation with myself
    which hides your presence from me.

Without you I am nothing, I can do nothing,
    but I trust in your mercy, my Father, my Creator.

Lord, you have searched me out and known me,
   you know my downsitting and uprising,
   you search all the thoughts of my heart.
Nothing is hid from you, my God and my All.

Lord, increase my love, that I may seek and find your love,
   the love you give to me.
Cleanse my memory and purify my mind,
   that I may pass beyond my own ideas of you
      to your very self,
   that you alone may fill my mind, memory and imagination.
Strengthen my understanding to bear the impress of your truth.
Enlarge my heart and draw all its longing
   into the one desire, to belong wholly to you.
Conform my will, that all my actions, thoughts and words
   may glorify you, my God, my Life and my All.

In your mercy, say within my soul, 'I am your salvation'.
My heart is open for you, say to my heart,
   'I am your saving health'.
My heart is small and narrow, but come into it,
   and by your coming enlarge it and dwell therein.
My soul is wounded,
   'Heal my soul, for I have sinned against you.'

Seraphim and Cherubim, the hosts of heaven,
Thrones, Dominions, Principalities and Powers,
Angels and Archangels declare your majesty.
   You created them and there is none like you,
      the Alpha and Omega, God Everlasting.

Praise be given you and glory be yours from every creature,
      O Truth Eternal,
      O loving Truth,
      O Eternal Love.

FIND

O God, you are my God, in you alone shall I find rest.

You are my God. You have given life to all creatures
   that they may offer back to you what you have given.
You are their Source and you uphold all their ways.
   The furthest star or the smallest atom,
   all have their form and origin in you,
      and do declare you to be their Creator.
Teach me to seek you for yourself, that I may find,
   and finding, love and worship you
      whose love has given me all things.

In the Word of God, the Light who lightens every man,
I may receive the light to find the remedy for my sinfulness—
   his Way, his Truth, his Life—the wonder of himself.
My Lord and my God, Christ, Son of God, have mercy.

We praise and thank you, Lord of Life,
   because you took our nature upon you,
   so that in every way, from birth unto death,
   you might be the perfect Humanity,
      to show forth God's saving truth.
   Lord Jesus Christ, have mercy.

We praise and thank you, Son of Man,
   for calling us and all men to follow you.
You are our Way and the Door to Life.
   Lord Jesus Christ, Son of God, have mercy.

Lord Jesus, born true man of Mary's virgin womb,
   in whom we see the Father manifest,
   whose grace sustains us in the Spirit's fellowship,
   draw us to find and to accept the good news of your love
   as we read and hear your saving word.
Most loving Saviour, Lamb of God, have mercy.
   Draw us that we may know and love you more.

At Bethlehem the angels sang, Glory to God on high,
good will to all who seek and find the unity of God and man.

> Lord, in your mercy, teach my soul
> that it may learn what you are to me.

Jesus, born in a stable for my sake,
> I worship you in your childhood.
Like the wise men I lay before you
> the gold of earth; its pomp and pride,
> the incense, which is the offering of my prayer,
> the myrrh, signifying my will to bear about
> > your dying, in my own life in this world.

Lamb of God, Son of God and Son of Man,
> you lead us on your way as pardoned captives,
> reclaimed by you from death,
> witnesses of your victory over sin,
> that we might spread abroad the knowledge of yourself.
We pray Lord, that we may know your love
> and witness faithfully to your love for all men.

By Jordan's waters where the Baptist's voice
> announced the day of judgement and of grace,
> my Lord was revealed as God's chosen Son.
Like the disciples then I ask, 'Rabbi, where are you staying?'
Invite me also to 'Come and see.'

> And in your mercy, teach my soul,
> that it may learn what you are to me.

The Lord of Life came to his own
> and they refused the love he gave.
His word remains as judgement to the end,
> yet he came to save and not to judge.
To those who accept he gives himself,
> the Bread of Life and the Cup of Salvation,
> > that we may dwell in him and he in us.

By him we are recreated in the Supper that enkindles love,
    with him we are offered to the Father's love,
    in him we are given the Spirit's fellowship,
        that we may do God's will.

On Calvary's hill, outside the city wall,
    despised, rejected by those he came to save,
Love offered up the perfect sacrifice of peace,
    himself the Victim, himself the Priest;
        uniting in one love God and man, in one true Personality,
            to glorify the Father's love who gave,
            to glorify himself, who gives,
                united in the Spirit's gift of unity.
    One full, perfect and sufficient,
    Oblation and Satisfaction for the sin of all the world.

        Lord, in your mercy, teach my soul,
            that it may seek and find and know
                all that you are to me.

All thanks and praise and glory be yours, O Lord,
    as we recognise you in the Breaking of the Bread.
Grant me to know you, and give myself wholly to you,
    as you give me a share in your own life,
        my Lord and my God, my Saviour, my Life and my All.

        *   *   *   *   *

KNOCK

Seek, find and knock: it is my Lord's command.

The way is straight. I must not swerve to seek an easy way
    nor cease to press on in the way, however dark it seems.

My hands stretch out to you, my soul is dry,
    like the thirsty land that waits for the rain.
It is my own self that darkens the way and hinders me
    from finding what I seek—the Love that calls to me—
    calls me to knock and wait until he answers me.
Lord, I am willing to go through fire and water
    if only I may come to the wealthy place
    where you will open to me the riches of your Heart.

Lord, I am content to knock and wait.
    You know what is best for me.
    Love's fire must purge and burn away my dross,
    the waters of redemption make clean what I have soiled.
It is your love which holds me to the door to knock
    when I am tempted to think, all is lost.
O God, you are my God, and the darkness
    which hides you is of myself and of the world.
O Lord, forgive the sins that cloud my sight.
    Increase my love to persevere in knocking.

Come, Holy Spirit, and pray within me
    as you take the things of Jesus and show them to me.
Inspire me to knock and knock again
    in faith's endurance, waiting at the door of love.
        Lord, have mercy.

Most Holy Spirit, the Comforter,
    to know you is to know the reality
    of union with Christ and with the Father.
        Lord, have mercy.

Christ himself is the Door of Life
    who, that we might come to him,
    knocks on the door of our heart.
If I open to him, freely, with all my heart,
    he will pour love into me, the love which is himself.
And I, receiving love, will give love in return,
      the love which he first gives to me.

My Lord, my God, my Life, my All.
You are both the Sower and the Seed sown in our hearts.
You are the Vine and we are the branches.
It is your desire that we should bring forth fruit
    and so be your disciples.
Your kingdom is not of this world,
    but it comes into this world.
When you set your face to go up to Jerusalem
    you asked your disciples, 'Who do you say I am?'
Lord, you are the Son of God, my Saviour and my King.

Have mercy upon me, receive my prayer,
    that I may follow faithfully
    and never fail to wait upon your word.
Lord, keep my heart steadfast,
    that I may witness to your presence within me.

IT SHALL BE OPENED

God, most wonderful in all your works,
    most worthy of adoration in your love,
        I worship you, I give you thanks,
    my Creator, Redeemer and Sanctifier.

God, three Persons in one Love,
    most holy Trinity of Unity,
        your glory is unique and claims my worship.
I praise your glory, I give you thanks,
    as I offer back to you the love
    which you have first given to me.

Lord Christ, your love draws all men to you.
    I worship you, I seek your face.
You have called us, each one,
    to be the Praise of your Glory
        in time and in eternity.

My soul would seek, find, knock;
    and would praise my God
    who created me and redeemed me
        and who wills to make me holy.

Lord, keep me steadfast in my love for you,
    my God and my All.

*   *   *

JOY IN GOD

CHRIST CALLS US to a life of conversion. He calls us to learn from him and to follow his way as his disciples. He does not look for a nominal adherence to a respectable and ordered religion; rather, he wants our complete dependence on him as our Saviour. He calls forth our complete self-giving and self-abandonment to him in love, and in this love he offers us union with himself. He came to save and not to judge, yet we are all the time under judgement through the word which he has spoken, and if we say we have no sin we deceive ourselves.

Our confidence is in Christ's love and his all-sufficient sacrifice for sin. In Christ we are offered to the Father, made acceptable in him by adoption and grace and indwelt by the Holy Spirit. Our salvation is all his work; it is his gift for he is 'not come to call the righteous, but sinners to repentance'. (Luke 5:32.)

We are the branches and he is the vine on whom we are dependent for our life and our fruitfulness. We are not justified by our works but by our faith in Christ. In fact, if our works are to be fruitful, they must arise out of our life in Christ. We so often put our works first and think of our prayer as a means to accomplish and forward the good that we would do. We are so troubled about many things that we forget the one thing necessary: our simple, loving dependence on Jesus.

Our prayer needs to contain these two basic elements of penitence and dependence. Penitence alone, without a sense of the mercy and love of God, and without confidence in his forgiveness, would be an unfruitful remorse. Likewise, our trust and dependence upon God, if it lacks the sense of our own falling far short of God's purpose for man, and our need of his forgiveness, is in danger of becoming arrogance. As we persevere in prayer, coming before God as we are and opening ourselves to be made what he would have us be, the Holy Spirit gives us true self-knowledge, and it is in the light of this knowledge of our dependence upon God and of our need of penitence that we may come to have a true knowledge of God.

Christ is our light and our salvation. It is his promise that if we keep his commandments his joy will be imparted to us, that our joy might be full.

MEN SEEK HAPPINESS: GOD OFFERS JOY

Lord God, you have made us your own.
My heart is not mine but yours
    and it is restless until it finds its rest in you.
My heart was given me that I might learn to love
    and to depend on him who gave me life.
Christ alone is the true end of my life.
    It is his joy that men should come to him
        that he may give them the love
           whereby they know his joy abiding in them
        so that he may be their joy fulfilled.

Lord Jesus Christ, you are 'He who is'
    and I am not, except I abide in you.
Most loving Lord, the Life and Light of men,
    teach me to grow in penitence,
    to realise I live only in you,
    so that, worshipping you, I may be ready
        to lose my life in this world
           if only I may find true and eternal life in you.
My Lord, my God, my Saviour and my Friend,
Jesus, who gives me life and forgives my sin,
    I praise and thank you for calling me
    to live within the kingdom of your love.
Jesus, if I seek for life and rest,
    I shall not find it in the world that passes on to death—
        but only in you—the Resurrection and the Life.
Your yoke is easy and your burden is light.
    I am indeed weary and heavy laden.
        Draw me to yourself.
           Give me rest and peace for my soul.

'Behold I stand at the door and knock.'
So Christ stands before the door of every soul.
    The hands with which he knocks are pierced;
    he will not force the human will.

His mercy waits, in meekness and lowliness of heart,
    for man to open the door and respond to his call.
He draws my soul by giving love, his love within me,
    so that I may answer and accept,
    in penitence acknowledging my sins.
He draws my soul to be dependent on his love,
    that he may free my soul to be his own,
    that I may use the things of earth as his and for him,
    so that my life, restored by grace, may be as he made it,
        the image and likeness of himself,
            that I may know, and men may know,
            he is my life, and I am his.

JESUS, to whom shall I turn but to you?
    For you have the words of eternal life.
JESUS, like the woman in the crowd I come to you
    to touch the hem of your garment.
JESUS, your love acknowledges every call;
    turn and look on me in answer to my faith.
JESUS, so patient with my sin, so just,
    that all must be disclosed, confessed;
    help me to grow in penitence,
    to recognise the deeds and thoughts
        that separate me from you.
    Make plain to me my falling-short,
        my sloth and carelessness, my care for worldliness,
        my respect for persons and fear of pain.
    O Lord, forgive all that I have done and do
        that wounds you in my fellow men.

JESUS, the faithful Shepherd of your flock,
    remember your Church.
Give her peace and unity,
    strengthen her power to witness to you.
Be present in those you call to martyrdom,
    make strong all who confess your Name.
Counsel those who bear responsibility for leadership.
Illumine the teachers, inspire the prophets,

confirm the faithful, be merciful to the sick and needy,
   that in their necessities each one may know your love
   ever present to uphold and help.
Lord of life, Love of men, Firstborn from the dead,
   praise, glory and power be yours
   from every creature and from all that you have made.

Lord Jesus Christ, have mercy.
   By your humility in taking flesh
   in order to remake the life of men
   I offer you myself, that you should take me for your own.
Lord Jesus Christ, have mercy.
   Through your Cross and Passion, Lord, I offer you myself.
   Draw me, good Lord, that I may hold fast to you.
Lord Jesus Christ, have mercy.
   In your promise to us, 'Lo, I am with you always',
   I offer you my prayer, that you will guide and heal.
Lord Jesus Christ, have mercy.

'Lift up your hearts.'
It is our duty and our joy that we should lift them to the Lord
   as we give him thanks and praise
   with angels and archangels and all the heavenly host.
      Holy, Holy, Holy, Lord God of power and might,
      heaven and earth are full of your glory,
         Hosanna in the highest.

Lord Jesus Christ, he that has seen you has seen the Father,
   and in you I may say, 'Abba', my Father.
Lord Jesus Christ, you have shown to us
   the brotherhood of man,
   that I may know and love my brother as myself.
Jesus, my Lord, your grace has been poured into my heart
   that it may be the Temple of the Spirit's fellowship.
Jesus, my Lord, you have broken down the dividing wall of sin
   and opened for us the way to the Father
   giving us access to him, with you, in the One Spirit.

'He who did not spare his own Son but gave him up for us all,
    will he not also give us all things with him?'

In you, O Lord, the saints are mine,
    your Mother and the blessed ones who see your Face.
The souls who rest in you, O Lord, are mine
    as they wait and pray for the completion of their joy.
In you, all those who wound and injure
        their fellow-men are mine,
    to love and hold to you for healing.
Jesus, my Lord, the sinners are mine,
    to offer you my prayer that they should turn to you.
All those who are in need are mine, in you, O Lord,
    the sorrowful, the heavy-laden and distressed.
Lord Jesus Christ, so fill my soul with your love
    that I may know the fulness of your life within me,
    that I may be transformed in mind and heart,
        to spend and be all spent,
        to give my love, which is your love in me,
    wherever you will that it should go.

Jesus, my Lord, watch over me, lest I fail to see your way,
    lest my love should fall short of your desire
    or be turned aside from your purpose for it.
Jesus, my Lord, watch over me, and when I stray,
    call me back. In penitence let me offer you my love again,
        more wholly and completely.

'Lift up your hearts.'
Christ reigns eternally and his love can never cease.
    His hands are pierced for love of me,
        they are stretched wide to draw me close.
    His heart beats for me,
        his love pours forth with power to heal.

God so loved the world that he gave his Son
    to be, in his manhood, the sacrifice for sin.
        Blood shed for many, blood shed for me.

Before the throne the Lamb stands as one slain.
He is worthy to receive blessing and honour
    with the Father and the Holy Spirit.
        Holy, holy, holy Lord, God of power and might,
        heaven and earth are full of your glory.
        Glory, my God, to you.

Jesus, I would lift up my heart to you
    that it may sing of your love
    repeating your Name in my love
    accepting all your way for me,
that I may learn your meekness and lowliness of heart
that I may find your yoke good to bear and your burden light,
    that I may be your true servant in this passing world,
        to glorify your Name;
    that with the angels and the saints
        I may sing for ever in the heavenly places
            Holy, holy, holy Lord, God of power and might,
            heaven and earth are full of your glory.
            Glory, my God, to you.

Lord Jesus Christ, I offer you my prayer for peace
    that your peace may be rooted in my heart
        and have such free course within me
    that I may offer it back to you
    that in your Church, divided by men's sins
        it may spread and make the unity for which you pray.
Lord Christ, the First and the Last, the Living One,
    I offer you my prayer for peace
        that in this world, full of tribulation,
        your hand may hold back the forces which divide,
    that men may seek to live in peace
    and may come repentant to your feet, to seek your peace.
Lord Christ, walking among the lampstands of your Church,
    you are the light and fire that burns in each.
You take the earthen vessels of our life
    and let your glory shine out through them.

I offer you my prayer for peace
    that I and each of those whom you have called
        purged by your loving fire, enlightened by your grace
    may come at last to be what you created us to be,
        the praise of your glorious love.
Lord Christ, I make my prayer to you,
    that my soul may be remade again,
        the clear mirror and image of yourself.
So increase my love, that you may see in me the true reflection
    of yourself, increasing from glory to glory
        as the Spirit transfigures my weakness.

Spirit of Love, your presence in my soul
    was purchased at so great a price by Christ my Lord.
    Inspire the thoughts of my heart
        that through prayer and penitence,
            by study and contemplation of the Word of Life
    I may be renewed and become one energy with you,
        penitent, dependent on your light.
Spirit of Love, who takes of the things of Jesus to show them to me,
    fill the darkness of my soul with your light
        that I may radiate your truth into the world's darkness.
Spirit of Love, strengthen my weakness,
    that dying to the world, I manifest Christ's light.

Lord Jesus, strengthen my will to pray
    that I may offer myself wholly to you
    as you draw me into your self-offering
        in Body broken and in Blood outpoured
    that I may belong wholly to you,
        my life filled with your love,
        my prayer inspired with energy to intercede,
that all the world may come to know the wonder of your love
    and to accept the healing you so long to give.

Wherefore, in peace let us pray to the Lord.
    For the peace which he alone can give,
        for the salvation of our souls,

for the unity of the Church, that it may be
> protected from error
> established in holiness
> witnessing truth:
for the peace of the world,
for the conversion of all men to the truth of God,
for the nations and peoples of the world
> that they may be made the Kingdom of our God;
for our friends and neighbours and for all our fellow-men,
> that they may be preserved in peace;
for all who travel, all who are sick or suffering,
for those departed from this life,
> that they may rest in peace.
Most mighty Lord, extend your mercy and your love
> to aid all those for whom we pray
> as we call to mind the blessed ones who see your Face,
> the Mother of God and all the saints.
Wherefore we commend ourselves and one another
> and our whole life to Christ our God.

To you, O Christ, I commend myself
> with all those who are mine in you, that we
> in the glory of the Father and the Spirit's fellowship
> may thank and praise you as we ought.
O Lamb of God, your power sustains me,
> you give life to all who turn to you.
You present the unity of human fellowship,
> a royal priesthood, kingdom and priests
>> before the Glory of the Unity of Trinity.

Blessing and honour and glory be yours
> now and for ever
> and unto the ages of ages. AMEN.

THE UNITY OF TRINITY

LOVE, OUR GOD, is a Trinity. Starting from our baptism into the Name of the Father and of the Son and of the Holy Spirit, this mystery of the Trinity is the very heart and foundation of Christian prayer. We recognise both the unity of God and the diversity of the work of the three Persons as they affect our lives and strengthen our response to the Love that creates, redeems and sanctifies us.

We need to make this affirmation of faith in the three Persons who are 'co-eternal together and co-equal' not just a cerebral exercise of our minds but a living reality in our experience of relationship with God. This is the work of prayer. As we contemplate the nature of each Person and the unity of each with the other, God will come to the aid of our weakness and lead us to a deeper knowledge of the mystery in love and worship.

We seek, we find, we grow in love as God gives us the increase of his love and as we persevere in surrendering ourselves to him in our dependence and penitence.

The arrangement of these prayers directs our attention first to the majesty of God in the uniqueness of his being and then to the mystery of this being as it is expressed in each Person. God is addressed by some of the titles which express the divine action. These words, such as, 'Sustainer' or 'Saviour', should not be passed over quickly, but dwelt upon and used slowly so as to draw out their full meaning, that this may give impetus to our thanksgiving and adoration.

Whenever we direct our attention to one of the Persons of the Trinity we shall find that this does not divide or separate from the unity; for each Person is completely one with and indivisible from the other Persons. As we direct our prayer to one of the Persons of the Trinity we shall find ourselves drawn into the relationship and interaction which exists between all three Persons in the unity of the Godhead.

Our desire to know the Father and to do his will draws us to the Son whom he gives as the perfect revelation of his being. Our love of the Son and our recognition of the full cost of the redemption he won for us helps us to appreciate more the greatness of the Father's love wherewith he loved us and sent his Son in the likeness of sinful flesh. Our knowledge of the Holy Spirit, as he shows us the things of Jesus, moves our wills to be more closely conformed to his image. The work of the Holy Spirit is always unifying; drawing us and all things into unity and drawing us back into the unity of the Godhead and the perfect relationship of mutuality between the Father, the Son and the Spirit.

As Christians, baptised into the Trinity, our inheritance is a genuine participation in this mutuality of the Trinity. But we have to claim this inheritance by our willing co-operation with God in our life of prayer and service, 'so that in all things the Unity in Trinity and Trinity in Unity' may be worshipped.

O GOD, you are my God,
>   I seek you with a heart that yearns for you.
> I seek your face; do not hide your face from me.

God is great and worthy of our praise,
>   there is no end of his greatness.

God the Father, Creator and Sustainer of all,
>   Fountain of life and Source of unfailing love,
>   have mercy upon us, whom you have made.
> God the Son, Saviour of the world,
>   our Shepherd, Priest and King,
>   our Friend and Brother, in whom we see the Father's face,
>   have mercy upon us, whom you have saved.
> God the Holy Spirit, filling all things with your power,
>   our Helper, Giver of light and Enkindler of love,
>   have mercy upon us, whom you fill with your life.
> Holy, Blessed and Glorious Trinity,
>   three Persons and One God,
>   have mercy upon us, who seek to know your love.

God our Father, you have given us faith and hope;
>   your love has flooded our inmost being.
> Teach us to answer your love with love.
>   My Lord and my God, increase my faith.
> Son of God, you promised to those who keep your word
>   that you would come with the Father
>   and make your home with them.
>   Even so, come to my heart, Lord Jesus.
>   My Lord and my God, draw my obedience back to you.
> Most Holy Spirit, you bring to our remembrance
>   the words of Jesus.
> Inflame our desire to give our hearts and minds and wills
>   to be refashioned after his likeness.
>   My Lord and my God, increase my love.

Father, Son and Holy Spirit, three Persons in One God,
   Creator, Redeemer, Sanctifier,
      hear us and have mercy upon us.

My God, you made me to reflect your life and your love
   but I have marred what you have made.
You know my unworthiness, my self-fulness,
   you know that I love you despite my sin
      and want to do your will.
   Only you can heal me and deliver me
      as you grant your forgiveness and give me new life.

The Father gave the Son in the power of the Spirit
   to draw all men back to him, their Creator.
The Son is our Way, our Truth and our Life.
In his own Person he reconciles all things.
   Draw me to follow your way of self-giving love.
The Spirit convinces me of sin and of righteousness
   and of my need for judgement.
Cleanse the hidden depths of my soul, that I may repent
   and be open to receive your Truth and Life.

God is Love, and in God all must be giving and receiving love.
   There is no end to love, for love is full relationship
      and in the evening of life all will be judged by Love.

Most Holy Spirit, one with the Father and the Son,
   fill my soul, that I may learn from you
      and love you present within me.
You never force the human will.
   Help me as I love and worship you
      to find the true liberty of obedience to your love,
      so that I may learn from you how to love
         and live according to your will.

My Lord and my God, I worship you,
   in majesty beyond all thought,
   in mercy drawing all men to yourself,

>   to know and depend on you in love,
>   because you made all men to worship you.
> Stir up my response to your love,
>   cleanse and inspire my inmost thoughts
>   so that in loving you in all men
>   I may come to be made one with you.
>
> My Lord and my God, how excellent is your mercy.
>   You are my hope and my prayer.
>   You have pity on the multitude of your people
>   in all times and in every place.
>   You send the rain of your mercy upon just and unjust.
>   You fill all things living with plenteousness.
>
> Give food to the hungry, comfort exiles and prisoners.
>   give quietness of mind to the distressed.
> Heal all sickness, multiply your blessings,
>   enliven your Church to be the faithful witness;
>   forgiving its divisions, bring about its unity.
> Strengthen your bishops in wisdom, vision and holiness,
>   increase your priests in number and in sanctity.
>   Help all Christians to be faithful to their calling
>   that confessing you before men fearlessly,
>   they may stand confessed by you,
>   before our Father in heaven.
>
> O Lord God, remember all those for whom we pray
>   with those for whom we may forget to pray
>   and those of whose needs we are ignorant.
> You know the needs of all; increase my love
>   that I may pray with deeper compassion and understanding,
>   that my prayer may convey your love to the whole world.
>
> We thank and praise you for all who love your Name,
>   for those who have become completely one with you in love;
>   for Mary, ever blessed Mother of God and all the saints.
> Unite our prayer with theirs, that all may glorify your Name.

Father, Son and Holy Spirit,
    mysterious Trinity and Unity of Love,
    I worship you, I praise you for your glory.
It is enough to say in awe and reverence,
    acknowledging the Unity in Trinity,
    God, you are God, everlasting, true God,
    holy, wonderful, nothing can compare with you.
You are beyond the conception of my mind
    but known in the depth of my heart.
O God you are my God,
    I worship you in Unity of Trinity.

I look upon the saving Cross,
    the Father's love that gave the Son,
    the Son's love in giving himself,
    the Spirit's love that sustains the sacrifice.

'The sacrifice acceptable to God is a broken spirit;
    a broken and contrite heart, O God, you will not despise.'
Love casts out the fear that is the punishment of sinful man.
Love draws the sinner to the tears of love,
    for his own sin and all the sin of men.
O Lord, forgive the wounds that we have made,
    for what we have done to any man we have done to you,
    and we shall have to look on you whom we have pierced.
Christ, uplifted on the Cross, draws all men to himself.
Christ is my life, in him all things are mine,
    if I depend on him alone, in penitence for sin,
        in love and faithfulness,
    that he may restore that which I lost—my unity with God.

Lord, give me love, that I may share the sorrow of your love
    and feel the wrongs men do unto men.
Lord, fill my soul with love, that I may know
    that you enfold me in your flock.
There is no limit to the breadth and length
    and height and depth of love.

Love draws all things to itself by Love's appeal.
Lord, so teach me in prayer to put love in where love is not
    that you may draw out love from those for whom I pray.
I worship you, Love incarnate.
Draw me to share your work of love and reconciliation,
    uniting man with creation, man with man
    and all things with God,
        making peace by the Blood of your Cross.

I praise and thank you in the offering of your love,
    the one, full, perfect and sufficient Sacrifice,
        Oblation and Satisfaction,
    wherein the scattered flock is made at one
    and power is given us to become the children of God.
Abba, Father, your children cry, your sons,
    reborn in the Son, filled with your Spirit.

Three Persons, one, all-holy God, very Love
    I praise and thank you for the wonder of your being.
Our fathers hoped in you, and we are called by your Name.
O Lord, we are but dust, and yet you make us alive.
O Lord, we are but strangers and pilgrims here on earth,
    yet you have made us fellow-citizens
        with the saints in heaven.
Teach me, O Lord, to live by faith, in expectant hope;
    increase my love, which is your love in me,
    that I may answer with my whole heart your Love's appeal.

Father, our Father enthroned in heaven,
    whose love gave to fallen man the Son, the Only-Begotten,
    that he should restore man, remade in him,
        to glorify you in the Unity of Trinity.
We worship and adore you as we acknowledge your Fatherhood
    wherein each one of us is remade to live and pray as sons,
        adopted brethren of your Son Jesus Christ.
In Christ we pray: Father, hallowed be your Name.

Lord Christ, the first and the last and the Living One,
    we consecrate ourselves to live in you,
        in the kingdom of your love,
    that reconciled and made your royal kingdom of priests
    we may be strengthened to do your will
        on earth as in heaven.
Lord Christ, who on the night in which you were betrayed,
    first gave yourself mystically to your disciples
        in the Bread and Wine, to make them holy,
    so may we ever obey your command
        to show forth your death until you come again;
            yourself our sacrifice and saving Bread,
            your Blood outpoured to wash away our sin.
We worship you as we proclaim the Mystery of Faith.

Healer, Sustainer, the only Source of life,
    conform my being to your likeness, renew my mind,
    transform my weakened will,
        that I may do what you would have me do.

My Lord and my God, you draw me to life.
You are more precious to me than all the goods of earth;
    how slow I am in making answer to your call,
    hesitant, wavering, uncertain and absorbed in myself.
How often I am faithless, lazy and disobedient,
    distracted by every passing attraction,
    taken up with the things that pass away.
In your mercy, pardon and forgive my sins and strengthen me.

You are the Peace in which alone I can rest secure.
If I fail to forgive those who injure me,
    I lose the capacity to receive your healing for my soul
        as I cling to the separations of lack of love within myself.
Fill my every thought with your love, that I may love,
    and loving, be forgiven of my sin.
Lead me in the way that I should go,
    and let me not be tested except with you.

Strong Deliverer, whose love has conquered death
    and overcome the evil that would separate
        the human soul from God,
   spare my weakness; let me not be overcome in the testings.
Deliver me from every evil, past, present and to come.
Keep my heart securely rooted in your love
    that with the saints I may praise you,
        in all circumstances,
           now and for ever.

Lord, I am not worthy that you should come
   to live within my soul and take me to yourself.
I am not worthy, Lord, yet you give yourself to me.
So fill my soul that I may love and persevere
    that at the end I may be found
        the loving servant of your love,
   to worship and adore eternally the Mystery of Love.
     Creator, Redeemer, Sanctifier,
        most Holy Trinity of Love,
           one God in Unity,
              my Love, my God.

THE FELLOWSHIP OF PRAYER

WHEN WE PRAY we do so as part of the Body of Christ and therefore our personal prayer can never be merely 'private' or individualistic. Prayer brings us into relationship with God and with all that God has made. When we pray we discover a fellowship with all the other members of the Body, living and departed, who also pray. We find the meaning of our lives in this relationship with other persons and with God as we open ourselves and our sympathy that others may live in and by us. We can do this because Christ himself lives in each one of us and we live in him. He has shown us the true glory of man so that we all 'reflect as in a mirror the splendour of the Lord; thus we are transfigured into his likeness from splendour to splendour'. (II Cor. 3:18.)

Our work is so to correspond with grace that we may perceive and give ourselves to that relationship in dependence upon him, in penitence for our rebellions and our falling short, both corporate and individual. Christ is the living Man who is the glory of God and we shall find the fulness of our own human personality in the richness of our fellowship with all other persons in him.

All that exists has its origin in God and comes to us as a gift. Jesus Christ has given himself to us in the Eucharist of his love. He is our Way. Our personal prayer depends on him and is part of the prayer of his Body the Church. By, with and in Christ, we are offered to the Father, and the Holy Spirit is given to us so that we pray in the very energy of God himself. We do well then to form our personal prayer upon the prayer of the Eucharist. Both should contain the same elements of meditation upon the word of God, petition, penitence, self-offering in union with the supreme oblation of Christ and thanksgiving. In both the Eucharist and personal prayer, through remembrance (*anamnesis*) of the Passion, Resurrection and Ascension of Christ and our calling down (*epiclesis*) of the Holy Spirit, we have access into the heavenly sanctuary 'by the blood of Jesus, by the new and living way which he opened up for us through his flesh'. (Heb. 10:19-20.) We have actual communion with Christ in the Eucharistic elements, and we need to assimilate them in our times of personal prayer in order that we may become what we are, and that our lives may be lived as members of his mystical Body. It is above all in the Eucharist that we experience also our fellowship with 'angels and archangels and the whole company of heaven', which is to be realised likewise in our personal prayer and in our lives. We are never so alone that we are not surrounded by the 'great cloud of witnesses' to faith who support us. (Heb. 12:1.)

Prayer is the humble seeking of a relationship in and through which we make our answer to God's love and by and in which we serve God. God has revealed himself to us and made for himself the earthly body of his Church so that we might make our response to his love, which first loved us, and that we might be found in him having the righteousness which comes from faith.

Let us therefore lift up our hearts to give thanks and praise, for in Christ's love we are no longer strangers and foreigners without a city, wanderers from place to place, but we are united in an unending fellowship with all the Saints of God.

THE LORD is my light and my salvation,
   He is the stronghold of my life.
Protect, O Lord, by the power of your Name
   those who follow you amid the tribulations of this world.
Consecrate them by your Truth
   and keep them from the Evil One,
     that they may look upon your glory,
      the glory given to you by the Father
       before the world began.
Glory be to the Word who took man's flesh
   that in his recreated manhood all mankind
     might be restored to union with God.
As the Father and the Son are one,
   the Father in the Son and the Son in us,
   we pray that we may be one with Christ in God,
     one with each other and with all men.
We praise and thank you, Lord of life,
   that you have gathered us all into one.
Your broken Body and your Blood outpoured
   heal the separations caused by sin.
     Christ, my Saviour, I worship and adore;
     help me to serve you and love you more and more.

For God alone my soul waits in silence
   for my hope is in him.
In truth he is my Rock of deliverance,
   my Tower of strength, so that I am unshaken.
All things come from God and on God all things depend.
   In God no man is solitary.
   In God he is one with all those who pray.
   In God he is one with all those who need prayers.
   In God he is one with those who rejoice
     and with those who are full of sorrow.
Lord, help me to see you in all men and all men in you
   that, opening my heart to you,

    you may pour out your love through me,
        that your will may be done in me
            and in all men,
    that all may be drawn to believe
that the Father sent the Son to be the Saviour of the world.
        Christ, my Saviour, I worship and adore,
            teach me to serve you and love you more and more.

Truly my heart waits silently for God.
    I trust in his steadfast love.
All things are made by God and loved by God;
all things are sustained and kept in being by God,
    and in God all things will come to completion.
Lord, show me my place in the unity of creation
    that I may die to my self-full separation
        and find my life in loving you
            and in loving my neighbour as myself.
Lord, help me to recognise all men as my brothers
    for we are all children of one Father.
Lord, help me to serve you and to serve my fellow-men
    that I may love and honour you
    in loving and honouring them.
        Christ, my Saviour, I worship and adore,
            draw me to follow you and love you more and more.

Teach me to wait on you alone
    and humbly to follow you with all my heart.
My Lord, my God, I know that anything good in me
    is all your work and not my own.
The more I know you as you really are
    the more I see myself for what I am,
        the more I know that I have only this self to offer
            that you should purify and cleanse it
            and make me what you would have me be.
My Lord, it is my desire, that your will should be done
    in me and through me, as perfectly as may be.
        Most loving Lord, my Saviour and my God,
        draw me to love you for yourself alone

because you are my God
and you made me for your own.

I will seek your face, O Lord;
   do not hide your face from me,
for in it I perceive the Father and yourself
   in the Spirit's fellowship of Trinity.
To know you I must know myself
   that here on earth I may be formed by you
   to do your will, so that my prayer may grow
   to become the splendour of the knowledge of yourself.
Lord, show me how I can be more wholly yours.

O God, make speed to save me, to help me.
   Save me from my own weakness and sinfulness.
   Save me from the power of hate and evil
      that would claim my soul and spirit.
   Save me from the Evil One
      who would make me a proud rebel, as he is.
O Lord, make haste to help me, to save me.
   Help me to know that I belong to you,
      redeemed, purchased from slavery to sin,
      by your saving Passion.
I trust in your mercy. Help me to believe that
   nothing in death or life
   nothing in the world as it is, nor in the world as it shall be,
   nothing at all, in all creation,
      can separate me from your love in Christ Jesus.

Jesus, who gave your life for me and conquered death;
Jesus, who lives for me, the Resurrection and the Life;
Jesus, who ever lives to plead on my behalf;
   take my life and live in me
   take my prayer and pray through me
   let my love and will be so one with yours
      that your kingdom may come
      your will be done on earth, and through me,
         as it is in heaven.

Jesus, let me learn by praying the splendour that is prayer,
> its energy and love,
>> which unites all those who pray in the fellowship of unity,
>> making us one with you in love
>> and one with all our fellow men.
Lord, let me know how you draw all men to yourself.
> Draw me, that I may open my heart to you.
> Support my prayer that it may become
>> a living, full relationship with you.

I thank you, Lord, that you have made me for yourself,
> that my heart may seek you.
I thank you, Lord, that you have claimed me for yourself,
> that I may serve you.
I thank you, Lord, that you give me yourself,
> your own very life, to keep me in life eternal.
My Lord, my Saviour and my Friend, I worship you,
> I am not worthy to receive you.
Lamb of God, triumphantly reigning in heaven,
> forgive my sin: grant me your peace.
Grant that I may be one with you in your love
> and made one in you with all that is;
>> that by you I may be remade, sharing your likeness,
>>> that I may grow up fully into you
>>> and come to share your own full stature,
>> O Christ, my Saviour and my God.

Lord, let my prayer be one with the offering of your Church
> and one with the prayer which you ever live to make
> that it may be acceptable to God the Father Almighty.
Lord, you have given me yourself;
> hide me under the shadow of your wings
>> lest I betray your grace
>> as I run the race that is set before me
>> and follow you on your Way.
A free heart will I offer you, O Lord, and praise your Name,
> because it is so full of your steadfast love.

Your Way, O Lord, is the Spirit's gift of liberty
 wherein, by giving and receiving love,
 each separate soul is made one with all.
 Holding fast the true freedom we have received
  we reflect as in a mirror the glory of your love.
 Receiving and reflecting love, becoming love,
  we are transfigured into your own likeness
   from splendour to splendour,
    by the work of the Lord who is Spirit.

Your Truth, O Lord, is the full perfection of love.
 Help me, O Lord, to know and act upon
  your truth of love in this my earthly life.
 Through the fellowship and discipline of your Church
  teach me your way of recreating love,
   that my human nature may be remade.
 As you love me and disclose yourself to me
  help me to receive your commands and obey them,
   that I may bear the fruit of love
    and so be your disciple.

Your Life, O Lord, is the unity of God and man.
 As limbs and organs of the Body of Christ
  man finds his life in you and you live in him.
 Lord, help me to understand the mystery of your Church,
  your living Body, Head and Members;
  how you keep it in the changing world
   suffering in the deformation of the times
   renewed and purified by persecution
    the faithful witness of your Name.
 Lord, give me grace that I may look to the end
  and know in you the very truth unshakeable:
   that fellowship remains when all the world passes away.

We often see our land as merely temporal
 yet its eternal inheritance in your saints
  remains to glorify your Name.

I praise and thank you, Lord of life,
    for all the souls made perfect in your love
      whose works we inherit
      and whose prayer continues to help us.
I commend myself and all men and all the life of men
      to Christ our God,
    that he will support us through the prayers
      made by his Mother and all the saints,
      for us and for all men,
    that we should be made perfectly one in his love.

Mary, Mother of God, revered by those who first built
    the wattled church at Glastonbury,
      pray for us.
Martyrs and Confessors of the Cornish lands,
      pray for us.
David of Wales and those who missionised the West,
      pray for us.
Oswald, who maintained the Faith unto death,
    remember those who die for Christ today
    with us who bear witness in our lives and
      pray for us.
Columba of the Isles, whose gentleness proclaimed the love of God,
      pray for us.
Margaret, whose place of prayer still crowns the rock of Edinburgh,
      pray for us.
Cuthbert, monk, bishop, evangelist and solitary,
      pray for us.
Gilbert, whose dying words proclaimed the mercy of God,
    'He does not sell, he gives, and gives to the poor',
      pray for us.
Edmund, most faithful unto death,
      pray for us.
Theodore, Dunstan and Thomas of Canterbury,
      pray for us.
Richard of Chichester, faithful shepherd of scattered sheep,
      pray for us.

Swithun of Winchester and Aldhelm of Malmsbury,
    pray for us.
Lord, as I recall the witness of your saints
    accept my prayer, uniting it with theirs.

O Lord, forgive the broken fellowship;
    forgive the wrongs men do to men;
    forgive the wrongs done in the name of religion;
    forgive the wrongs done in the past and still done
        in your own Name, when men forget
        you laid down your life
    to make peace by the Blood of your Cross,
    to make man one with his fellow-men
        and one with God.

Lord, you save us when all that man can do must fail.
    In these days of violence and hatred,
    when man destroys his fellow man
        both in body and in mind
    by bombs and torture and the misuse of drugs;
    help us to know our fellowship with all the saints
       with those made perfect by suffering,
        who, wholly one with you, watch over our way.
Grant us to know their prayer of love supports our way
    and helps us to put love in where love is not
    that we and they may glorify your Name.

As the sound of many waters,
    vibrant, filling all consciousness,
    so is the praise of Unity
    that moves the soul in unison with heaven's song,
        unheard, unseen, yet known,
    to praise the Lamb and bless his Name.
My Lord, my God, my King, I worship you.
All things, all men, all time and every place are yours.
You are the Lamb of God, whose sacrifice brings peace.

By your free-willed self-offering, yourself the Priest,
   you have broken down the dividing wall of sin,
      making God and man at one
   that in the end, all shall be well.

Lord, may my knowledge of the fellowship
   in the communion and union of prayer
      move my desire to pray and love you more.
O Lord, strengthen and deepen my prayer,
   that your love in me may increase,
      to draw all men back to you.
   May we all grow to love you more
      till all be perfect Unity,
         a fellowship unbreakable in Love's desire
           to know and serve and glorify you,
              my Lord and my God.

                                        AMEN

THE FACE OF LOVE, Meditations on the Way of the Cross by Gilbert Shaw. Revised edition SLG Press, 1977. Price: £1.75

In her review of the first edition, published in 1959, Julia de Beausobre wrote in a *Mowbray's Journal* of that year:

> The author does not seek to dictate a method or words of prayer, but hopes to help others, less conversant with affective prayer than he is, to build up a solid Christian disposition of mind and emotion. He may touch off a soul's desire for greater conformity with the Divine Will at all times and in all places ... With appositeness and a pleasing sureness of touch he uses many rhythms of poetry and prose, or the prose of matter-of-fact statement ... A theme emerges, takes the lead, is superseded, yet echoes on. But the impetus is towards 'the fulness of adoption' where concepts vanish and words cease.
>
> The exercises are rooted in experience so tempered as to be helpful to many, however inexperienced. Passages best suited to individual needs can easily be singled out; they may vary with time or occasions. Through the valley of the shadows of love they trace with firm delicacy God's unalterable ways for the redemption of men.

This second edition is a tribute to a great lover of God, the main motive of whose priestly ministry was prayer and witness to the life of reconciliation. Hence the theme of the book, as Gilbert Shaw himself says in the Introduction, is 'to bring the Passion of our Lord into relation with the situations of our time and our practical dealings with life.' Many will find it an unerring guide into the prayer of contemplative intercession.

From the Foreword by MOTHER MARY CLARE SLG

OTHER SLG PUBLICATIONS BY GILBERT SHAW

A PILGRIM'S BOOK OF PRAYERS	£1.20
SITIO (I THIRST) Intercessory Prayers	.90
RHYTMIC PRAYERS	.25
CHRISTIAN PRAYER: A WAY OF PROGRESS	.30
CREATION AND RE-CREATION: An Approach to Prayer	.30
THE CHRISTIAN SOLITARY	.15